ESSENTIAL **DK** COMPUTERS

ELECTRONIC PUBLISHING

DESKTOP
PUBLISHING

D0921656

ABOUT THIS BOOK

Desktop Publishing is for people who are familiar with Microsoft® programs for the PC and who want to make use of Publisher 2000 to design and publish their own work.

THIS BOOK CONCENTRATES ON THE facilities that Microsoft® Publisher 2000 offers for creating and designing publications with a small-to-medium-sized distribution. If you want to produce newsletters, handbills, or other small-run publications, Publisher is the ideal tool. This program offers complete control over the layout and positioning of text and images on the page, a wide range of facilities for moving, coloring, and shaping text, and the ability to import images in many formats. Related topics are grouped together in chapters for an easier understanding of what actions are possible in Publisher and how to carry them out. These build on previous explanations so your knowledge is developed through a logical sequence.

The chapters and the subsections use a step-by-step approach. Virtually every step is accompanied by an illustration showing how your screen should look at each stage. The screen images are either full-screen or focus on an important detail that you'll see on your screen. If you work through the steps, you'll soon start feeling comfortable that you're learning and making progress.

The book contains several features to help you understand both what is happening on screen and what you need to do. A labeled Publisher window is included to show the important elements that are used in Publisher. This is followed by an illustration of the toolbars, at the top of the screen, to help you find your way around these invaluable, but possibly perplexing, controls.

Cross-references are shown in the text as left- or right-hand page icons: ⌐ and ⌐. Page numbers and references are shown at the foot of the page.

In addition to the step-by-step sections of the book, there are also boxes that describe and explain particular features of Publisher in detail, and tip boxes that provide alternative methods, shortcuts, handy hints, and how to get out of trouble. Finally, at the back of the book, you will find a glossary explaining new terms and a comprehensive index.

Publisher 2000 offers complete control over the appearance and layout of your document.

ESSENTIAL DK COMPUTERS

ELECTRONIC PUBLISHING

DESKTOP PUBLISHING

JOSHUA MOSTAFA

A Dorling Kindersley Book

Dorling Kindersley
LONDON, NEW YORK, SYDNEY, DELHI,
PARIS, MUNICH, and JOHANNESBURG

Produced for Dorling Kindersley Limited by
Design Revolution, Queens Park Villa,
30 West Drive, Brighton, East Sussex BN2 2GE

EDITORIAL DIRECTOR Ian Whitelaw
SENIOR DESIGNER Andy Ashdown
PROJECT EDITOR John Watson
DESIGNER Paul Bowler

MANAGING ART EDITOR Nigel Duffield
SENIOR EDITOR Mary Lindsay
DTP DESIGNER Jason Little
PRODUCTION CONTROLLER Wendy Penn

Published in the United States by Dorling Kindersley Publishing, Inc.
95 Madison Avenue, New York, New York, 10016

First American Edition, 2000

2 4 6 8 10 9 7 5 3 1

Copyright © 2000 Dorling Kindersley Limited, London
Text copyright © 2000 Dorling Kindersley Limited, London

Screen shots of Microsoft® Publisher 2000 used
by permission from Microsoft Corporation.

All rights reserved under International and Pan-American Copyright
Conventions. No part of this publication may be reproduced,
stored in a retrieval system, or transmitted in any form or by any means,
electronic, mechanical, photocopying, recording, or otherwise,
without the prior written permission of the copyright owner.

Published in Great Britain by Dorling Kindersley.

A catalog record is available from the Library of Congress.

ISBN 0-7894-6893-X

Color reproduced by First Impressions, London
Printed in Italy by Graphicom

For our complete
catalog visit
www.dk.com

CONTENTS

MICROSOFT PUBLISHER

Publisher is a complete desktop publishing program that is
capable of handling documents that vary greatly in size and
complexity, and which is easy to learn and very flexible.

WHAT CAN PUBLISHER DO?

Publisher gives you all the tools you need
to create your own publications –
newsletters, advertising and promotional
material, greetings cards, or any of a host
of others – straight from your PC and
printer. You can integrate graphics into
your text and text into your graphics and,
even if you have no publishing experience,
you have complete control over the layout
of each page in every publication you
produce. You can, in effect, design and
create your page to take on exactly the
appearance that you want, and with a
minimum of effort.

WHAT IS A PUBLISHER DOCUMENT?

The documents that you
create using Publisher are
called *publications*. A
publication can be many
pages or simply one page,
and usually contains text,
graphics, and all the
formatting you have added.
These are stored on your
computer's hard disk and
can be printed out using
your desktop printer, or by
using a commercial
printing service.

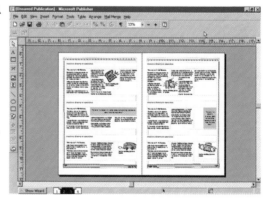

Packing files for
a print service
59

LAUNCHING PUBLISHER

Publisher launches like any other Windows program. With the Windows desktop on screen, you can launch

Publisher as the only program running, or you can run it alongside other software to exchange data with other applications.

1 LAUNCHING BY THE START MENU

● Place the cursor over the **Start** button on the Taskbar and click with the left mouse button.
● Move the cursor up the pop-up menu until **Programs** is highlighted. A submenu of programs appears to the right.
● Move the cursor down the menu to **Microsoft Publisher** and left-click again. (If Microsoft Publisher is missing from the Program menu, it may be under Microsoft Office.)
● The Microsoft Publisher window opens ⌐.

2 LAUNCHING BY A SHORTCUT

● You may already have a Publisher icon on screen, which is a shortcut to launching Publisher. If so, double-click on the icon.
● The Microsoft Publisher window opens ⌐.

8 The Publisher Window

THE PUBLISHER WINDOW

If you're familiar with Microsoft programs, such as Word 2000, the Publisher window will look very familiar. The most obvious difference is the Objects toolbar down the left of the screen. If you are new to Microsoft programs, you will find that Publisher is one of the easiest desktop publishing packages to learn.

THE PUBLISHER WINDOW

❶ Title bar
❷ Menu bar
Contains the main menus
❸ Toolbars
Buttons for common Publisher actions
❹ Horizontal ruler
Used for measuring distances across the page
❺ Blank page
New blank page in a publication
❻ Up scroll button
Moves the display up the page
❼ Vertical scroll box
Click and drag this to move quickly up or down the page of the publication
❽ Vertical scroll bar
❾ Down scroll button
Moves the display down through the page
❿ Right scroll button
Moves the display of the publication in increments across the page

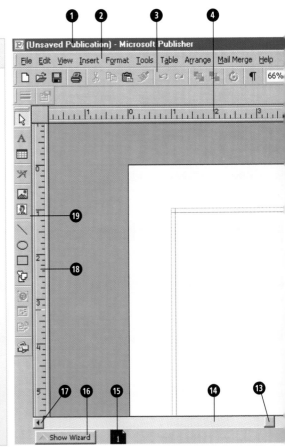

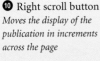

POSITIONING TOOLBARS

The toolbars don't have to appear on the top of your page. They can "float" freely anywhere in your publication, and you can move them out of the way if you need to. Just click on the raised ridge at the left-hand end of a toolbar and drag it to a new location.

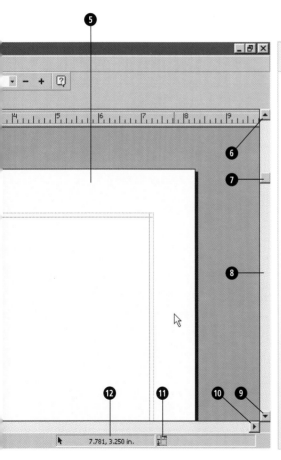

THE PUBLISHER WINDOW

⓫ Object Size
Displays the size of the currently selected object in the publication

⓬ Object Position
Location of the mouse pointer, or the currently selected object

⓭ Horizontal scroll box
Click and drag this to move quickly across the page

⓮ Horizontal scroll bar

⓯ Page icons
Used to select and display pages

⓰ Show Wizard button
Displays the currently used wizard

⓱ Left scroll button
Moves the display left across the page

⓲ Vertical ruler
For measuring vertical distances

⓳ Objects Toolbar
For adding objects to your page

7.781, 3.250 in.

THE PUBLISHER TOOLBARS

The most frequently performed tasks are available via the Publisher toolbars. The Objects toolbar is positioned vertically down the left-hand side and is used for inserting objects such as text frames, scanned photos, and clip art drawings.

The Standard toolbar allows you to perform basic functions such as opening or saving publications at a single click. The Formatting toolbar changes its options depending on what kind of object you are currently working on.

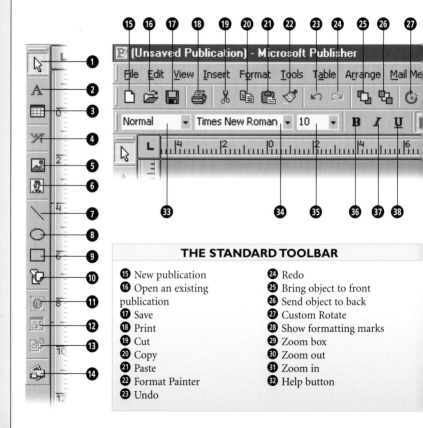

THE STANDARD TOOLBAR

15 New publication
16 Open an existing publication
17 Save
18 Print
19 Cut
20 Copy
21 Paste
22 Format Painter
23 Undo
24 Redo
25 Bring object to front
26 Send object to back
27 Custom Rotate
28 Show formatting marks
29 Zoom box
30 Zoom out
31 Zoom in
32 Help button

THE OBJECTS TOOLBAR

1. Pointer
2. Text frame
3. Table frame
4. WordArt frame
5. Picture frame
6. Clip gallery
7. Line
8. Oval
9. Rectangle
10. Custom shapes
11. Hot Spot
12. Form Control
13. HTML code fragment
14. Design Gallery object

ScreenTip
It isn't necessary to memorize all these buttons. Roll the cursor over a button, wait for a second, and a ScreenTip appears telling you the function of the button.

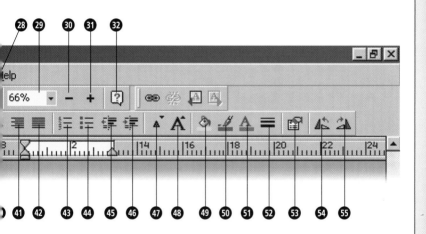

66%

THE FORMATTING TOOLBAR

33. Style selector
34. Font selector
35. Font size selector
36. Bold
37. Italic
38. Underline
39. Left-aligned text
40. Centered text
41. Right-aligned text
42. Justified text

43. Numbered list
44. Bulleted list
45. Decrease indent
46. Increase indent
47. Decrease font size
48. Increase font size
49. Fill color
50. Line color
51. Font color
52. Line/border style

53. Text frame properties
54. Rotate left
55. Rotate right

PUBLISHER WIZARDS

When you first launch Publisher, the **Microsoft Publisher Catalog** appears, which contains a number of wizards.

A wizard is a tool that can take you step-by-step through the essential elements of producing different types of publication.

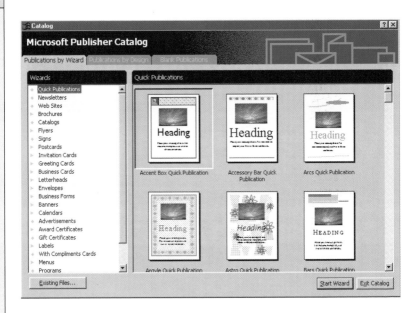

BY WIZARD OR BY DESIGN?

● The first tab, **Publications by Wizard**, contains numerous wizards to help with particular kinds of publications. The second tab, **Publications by Design,** lists the wizards according to their style.

BLANK PUBLICATIONS

● The third tab, **Blank Publications**, can be used to create your own publications containing your own design, but with sophisticated layouts, which allow paper and card to be folded and presented in a variety of ways.

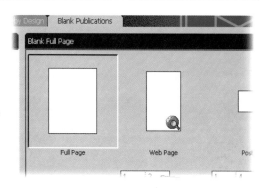

EXITING THE CATALOG

● Wizards are dealt with in a chapter later in this book ⌐ when the principles of how Publisher works have been looked at.

● To get to a new Publisher document, or *publication*, click on **Exit Catalog** at bottom right of the window, and on **Hide Wizard** at bottom left.

BLANK PUBLICATIONS

● Your screen should now show a blank page with its associated rulers and toolbars, ready to be worked on.

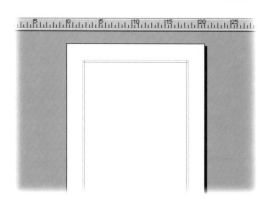

MOVING AROUND PUBLICATIONS

It is easy to navigate your way around a Publisher publication. You can zoom in and out, move between pages, and move within pages. Also, the PgUp and PgDn keys work as usual, and the Home and End keys function within text boxes.

1 ZOOMING IN AND OUT

- You can change the view of your publication via the plus and minus buttons to zoom in and out.
- Alternatively, you can enter a display percentage in the Zoom box.

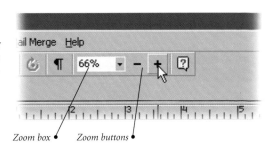

Zoom box •   *Zoom buttons* •

2 MOVING BETWEEN PAGES

- If your publication has more than one page, you can move between pages by clicking the page icons at the foot of the screen.
- Click on the icon of the page icon to move to.

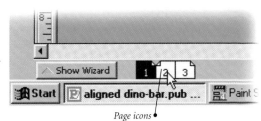

Page icons •

3 MOVING AROUND THE PAGE

- If you have zoomed in too far to see the whole page on the screen, you can use the scroll bars to view different areas of your page.
- Drag the scroll box with the mouse to move up and down the page.

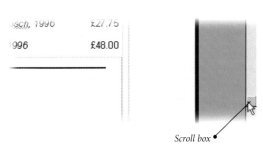

Scroll box •

SAVING YOUR PUBLICATION

As with all computer applications, it's important to save your work regularly. If you decide to use an old publication and make changes to it to create a new one, make sure you save your new publication under a new name to keep both versions.

1 THE SAVE AS COMMAND

● Click on **File** on the Menu bar and click on **Save As**.

● After the first save, use **Save** from the **File** menu.

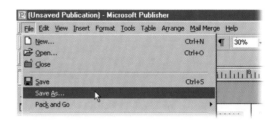

2 NAMING YOUR FILE

● The **Save As** dialog box opens on screen.

● Place the insertion point in the **File name** box, and type a name that you will remember it by.

● Click on **Save**.

3 RECALLING YOUR FILE

● Drop down the **File** menu and click on **Open**.

● The Open dialog box appears. Navigate to your file and click on **Open**.

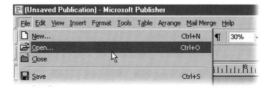

ADDING TEXT

If you are used to using Word 2000, you might find it puzzling that you cannot simply begin typing in Publisher. Text areas have to be defined first, as does each element that you insert.

TEXT FRAMES

To add text to a publication, first create a *text frame*, which is an area on a page that contains only text. You can type directly into a text frame from the keyboard, or insert text from existing files. To begin with, we will use the keyboard.

1 THE TEXT FRAME TOOL
● With the text frame tool you can place a text frame exactly where you need it to be on the page.
● Click on the text frame tool, the cursor changes to a cross hair as you move it onto the window.

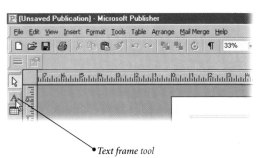

●*Text frame tool*

2 DRAWING THE TEXT FRAME
● Click where you want one corner of your text frame to appear, and drag the cursor to the opposite corner position.
● Release the mouse button and the text frame appears on the page.

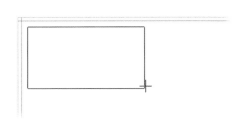

3 ENTERING TEXT

● At this point, the
Formatting toolbar appears
at the top of the screen as
well as the four buttons
related to connecting and
moving to text frames ⌐.
● The insertion point is
blinking in the top left-
corner and you can begin
entering text.

The writing is on the wall

4 RESIZING THE TEXT FRAME

● Click inside the text box
to select it, and place the
cursor over one of the
handles. The arrow cursor
changes to the resize cursor.
● Click and drag the frame
to resize it.

The writing is on the wall

The Resize cursor ●

5 MOVING THE TEXT FRAME

● Move the mouse over
any of the lines marking
out the text frame.
● The move cursor appears
and you can click and drag
to move the frame.

The writing is on the wall

The Move cursor ●

USING WORD

When you're entering text, you may prefer to be able to see your words uncluttered by the surrounding details of your publication – and fit the text later into the the design. With Publisher you can create your text by using Microsoft Word 2000.

1 LAUNCHING WORD

● Select the text frame by clicking within the borders.
● Drop down the **Edit** menu and select **Edit Story in Microsoft Word**.
● Microsoft Word opens with your text in a new document.
● Type in your text or edit what was already in the text frame.

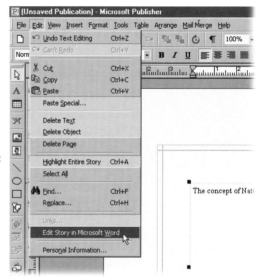

What is a story?
In Publisher, any continuous piece of text is known as a story. As you can divide text between frames, possibly on different pages, the word story is used to make it clear that the text forms a continuous narrative.

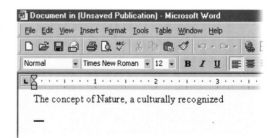

2 EDITING THE TEXT

● All the editing and formatting features that Word contains can be used to create the contents and appearance of your text.

● Publisher is able to import text created using Word and reproduce it exactly as it appeared in the Word document.

The concept of Nature, a culturally recognized and shared order with claim to universal as well as social scope, is a contentious one charged with political, social, scientific, aesthetic, and philosophical implications.

3 RETURNING TO PUBLISHER

● When you have edited your text, drop down Word's **File** menu and select **Close & Return to (Unsaved Publication)**.

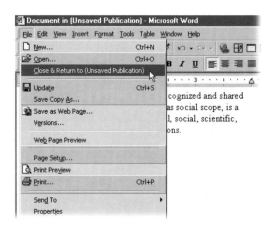

● Word closes and the text
you have been working on
reappears in the text frame
in your publication.

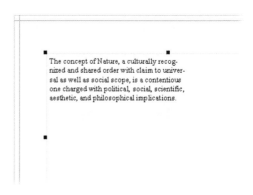

The concept of Nature, a culturally recognized and shared order with claim to universal as well as social scope, is a contentious
one charged with political, social, scientific,
aesthetic, and philosophical implications.

USING EXISTING FILES

You may already have created pieces of
text for your publication and saved them
to disk. Publisher can import text that has
been created in any of a number of
different document formats and insert
it into a text box in the publication.

1 INSERTING TEXT

● Make sure you have your
text frame selected.
● Drop down the **Insert**
menu and select **Text File**.

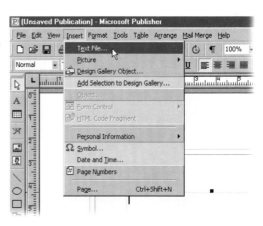

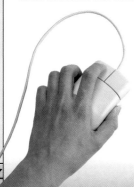

2 CHOOSING THE FILE

● The **Insert Text** dialog box opens.

● Navigate to the file containing the text that you want by clicking on the arrow to the right of the **Look in:** box and locating the folder containing it.

● Highlight the file and click on **OK**.

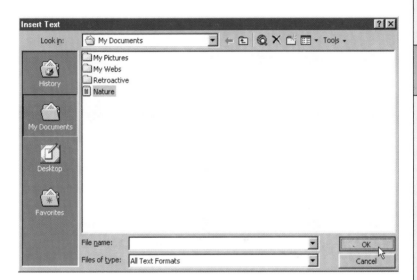

● The text from the file is now inserted into the text frame on your publication.

The concept of Nature, a culturally recognized and shared order with claim to universal as well as social scope, is a contentious one charged with political, social, scientific, aesthetic, and philosophical implications, A striking characteristic of the fin de siècle is its breaking away from Victorian values and rejection of the assumed natural order.

CONNECTING FRAMES

If you have a large amount of text in one *story*, or section of text, it may not fit into one text frame. In Publisher, it is easy to distribute your text across two or more frames by connecting them. Once connected, you can move, resize, and edit the text, which will be automatically adjusted across the linked text frames.

1 SELECT THE FIRST FRAME

● When you have inserted more text than the frame can display, the **Text in Overflow** indicator appears below the text frame.

● Place a second, empty text frame into the publication, then select the first frame by clicking on it.

● Make sure the frame is selected and drop down the **Tools** menu.

● Click on **Connect Text Frames** on the menu.

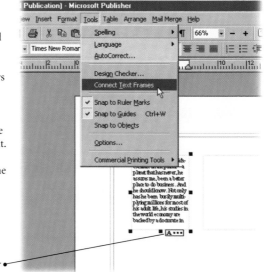

*The **Text in Overflow** indicator* ●

ALTERNATIVES TO ADDING A FRAME

Sometimes, adding more text frames is not the solution because, for example, you have insufficient room. You may, however, have enough space to increase the text frame by selecting it and dragging one of its handles into the free space. You could decrease the font size by selecting the text and choosing a size from the **Font Size** box. If you have margins in a text frame, you could make them smaller by selecting **Text Frame Properties** in the **Format** menu and enter new margin settings in the **Margins** section.

2 POURING IN THE TEXT

● Your mouse pointer becomes an overflowing pitcher icon.

● Click on the text frame into which you want to pour the text.

● The text now flows from one frame to the next.

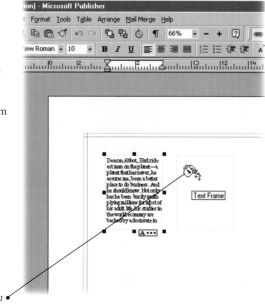

Pitcher to pour in text

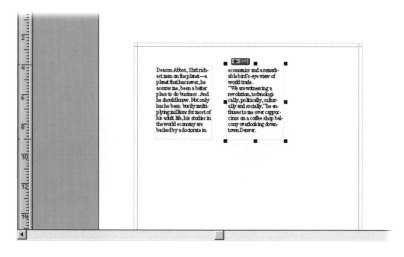

ADDING GRAPHICS

Words on their own are only half the story. No publication is complete without graphics, which are available from numerous sources: clip art, images from the Internet, or your own images.

CLIP ART

If you need simple, striking, and colorful images to illustrate the subject matter of your publication and to make the appearance more lively, you may need to look no further than the clip art that comes bundled with Publisher.

FINDING CLIP ART

● Click on **Insert** on the Menu bar. The **Insert** menu drops down.
● Click on **Picture** and a submenu opens.
● Select **Clip Art** from the submenu, and the Clip Gallery is made available.

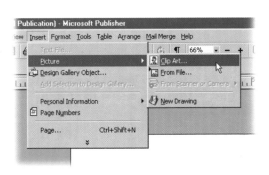

CHOOSING CLIP ART

Once you have entered the Clip Gallery, you will find that the images are organized into a large number of categories. You can find clips by choosing a category, by searching using everyday language, or by finding clips similar to a clip that you've found, but isn't exactly what you're looking for. You're not limited only to the images available in the Clip Gallery. From the Clip Gallery you can link to a special website and, if you select any clips from the site, they are automatically added to your own Clip Gallery.

IMAGE FILES

In addition to the clip art provided through the Clip Gallery, you can also insert other images into your publication.

Publisher can handle a wide variety of image file formats, which allows you to use your own image files.

1 INSERTING AN IMAGE FILE

● Drop down the **Insert** menu and click on **Picture**. A submenu appears.

● Click on **From File** in the submenu.

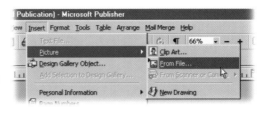

2 CHOOSING YOUR IMAGE FILE

● The **Insert Picture** dialog box opens.

● Navigate through your folders to find the image file you want.

● Click once on the file to select it, and an image of what the file contains is shown in the preview panel. Click on **Insert**.

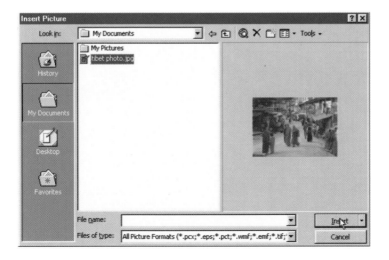

● Your image will appear on the page.

● To position the image, place the cursor over it, hold down the left mouse button, and simply drag the image until it reaches the required position.

RESIZING AN IMAGE

It is unlikely that an image will be the size you want. However, you can resize your images to fit particular spaces on your page. Be careful when resizing because

bitmap image files (that is, any file with a name ending in jpg, pcx, wmf, or bmp) will appear to be made up of large blocks of color if you enlarge them too far.

RESIZING IN PROPORTION

● To keep your picture the same shape while you resize it, place the cursor over one of the handles at a corner.

● The **Resize** pointer appears. Hold down the left mouse button and drag away from, or toward, the opposite corner.

● Release the mouse button when the image is the size you want.

● *Resize* pointer

ROTATING AN IMAGE

Rotation is a frequently used design tool that adds impact. In Publisher, you can rotate images, text, or any object that you have inserted into your publication. Here we will see how to rotate images. To rotate WordArt text ⬒ to match, see page 49 ⬒.

ROTATING AN IMAGE MANUALLY

● Select the image by clicking on it.
● Hold down the [Alt] key on your keyboard and position the cursor over one of the handles. The cursor changes to the rotation pointer.

● Hold down the left mouse button and drag the pointer. An outline frame appears indicating the degree of rotation. You can now release the [Alt] key.
● When the outline frame has reached the required angle, release the mouse button and the image is rotated on the page.

46 **WordArt**

49 **Rotating Your Text**

CROPPING AN IMAGE

If you want to show only a part of your image, you can remove the unwanted part by using Publisher's crop tool. Although it appears that you've cut out part of the image, the unwanted part is still there – all you're doing is hiding it.

CROPPING AN IMAGE

● Begin by clicking on the image to select it, then click on the **Crop Picture** button in the toolbar.

● Place the cursor over one of the sizing handles and the cropping tool appears.

● Hold down the left mouse button and drag the cropping tool over the image. A dotted line appears to show how much is being cropped.

● When finished, release the mouse button and click on the **Crop Picture** button to cancel the cropping tool.

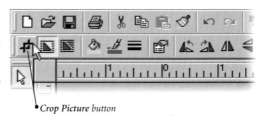

●*Crop Picture button*

●*Cropping tool*

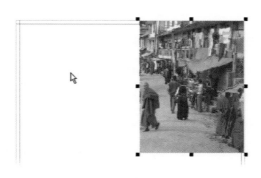

WRAPPING TEXT AROUND IMAGES

To integrate your graphics more fully into your text, break up blocks of text, or to make a feature out of irregularly shaped graphics, you can wrap text around the images on your page, so the images are nestling within the words of the text.

1 INSERT THE IMAGE

● Insert an image file 📄.
● Position it over a text frame so that it eclipses part of the text. (If the image is behind the text, press F6 to bring it to the front 📄.)

2 WRAP TEXT TO PICTURE

● Click on the **Wrap Text to Picture** button on the toolbar.

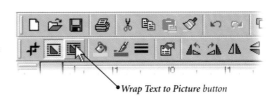

●*Wrap Text to Picture button*

● The text wraps tightly around the image instead of just the frame in which it sits.

PUBLICATION LAYOUT

In this section, your publication will start to take shape as we look at how the objects on the page work with each other, and how the pages come together to form the publication.

ALIGNING OBJECTS

So far we have been looking at how to position objects on the page manually, and handling each object separately. But it would be a very laborious process if each individual object had to be aligned with other objects by hand and it all had to be done using the mouse. Fortunately, with Publisher, it is possible to align objects with each other in several ways – and with absolute precision.

1 SELECTING THE OBJECTS

● First, select the objects you wish to align by holding down the ⇧ Shift key and left-clicking on each one in turn.
● Right-click on any of the selected objects to open a pop-up a menu.
● Click on **Align Objects**.

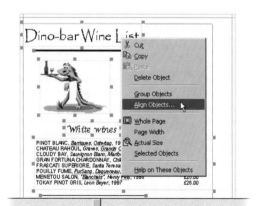

2 ALIGNING LEFT TO RIGHT

● The **Align Objects** dialog box opens.
● To align your objects

along one side, click one of the alignment options under **Left to right**.
● You can align objects flush against the page

margin with the **Align along margins** check box.
● Click on **OK**.
● Your objects are now aligned along one side.

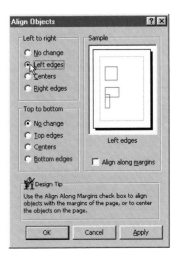

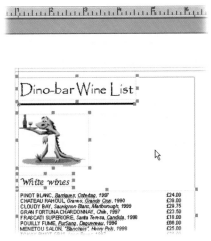

3 ALIGNING TOP TO BOTTOM

● Now try aligning top to bottom. Select several objects that are side by side on your page.
● Go through steps 1 and 2, but click on one of the options under **Top to bottom** in the **Align Objects** dialog box.
● Click on **OK**.

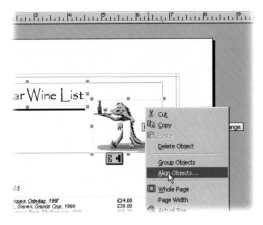

● The top edges of your selected objects are now aligned with one another.

GROUPING OBJECTS

Some objects are always fixed in relation to one another. For example, a picture frame containing a company logo and the text frame with the company name may always stay side by side. You can tell Publisher to *group* selected objects. The objects are then treated as a single unit on which commands can be carried out.

1 SELECTING OBJECTS

● Hold down the ⬆Shift key and select the objects you wish to group by single-clicking on each one in turn.
● The **Group Objects** button appears next to one of the objects.
● Click on this button and the selected objects are now grouped.

Group Objects button ●

White wines	
PINOT BLANC, Barriques, Ostertag, 1997	£24.00
CHATEAU RAHOUL Graves, Grands Crus, 1990	£39.00
CLOUDY BAY, Sauvignon Blanc, Marlborough, 1999	£29.75
GRAN FORTUNA CHARDONNAY, Chile, 1997	£23.50
FRASCATI SUPERIORE, Santa Teresa, Candida, 1998	£18.00
POUILLY FUME, PurSang, Daguereau, 1996	£66.00
MENETOU SALON, "Banchais", Henry Pelé, 1998	£25.00
TOKAY PINOT GRIS, Leon Beyer, 1997	£26.00

Red wines	
CABERNET SAUVIGNON, Vista Andes, Argentina, 1997	£14.95
CHATEAU RAHOUL Graves, L'Union des Grands Crus, 1991	£36.50
FLEURIE, Chateau Des L'Abourons, 1997 (available chilled)	£25.00
CHATEAU MUSAR, Bekaa Valley, Lebanon, 1991/93	£35.00
ALAMOS RIDGEMALBEC, Alamos Ridge, Argentina, 1996	£18.00
MULDERBOSCH, Faithful Hound, Cabernet, Stellenbosch, 1996	£27.75

2 MOVE GROUPED OBJECTS

● Click on any of the objects and drag with the mouse to move all the elements that make up the group.

● You can resize the entire group as one object.

Move cursor

3 UNGROUPING OBJECTS

● When you click on a collection of previously grouped objects, the **Group Objects** button has changed and is now the **Ungroup Objects** button.

● To ungroup the objects, for example, if you want to move or resize them separately, or create a new group, click on the **Ungroup Objects** button.

Ungroup Objects button

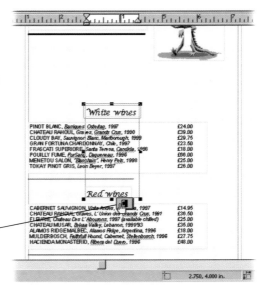

LAYERING OBJECTS

If two objects overlap, one will always be *on top* of the other. Publisher places objects on invisible *layers* – with each new object occupying a higher layer than the objects created before it. But you have complete control over altering the layers.

1 SELECTING AN OBJECT

● In this example, the name is obscuring the logo because it was created after the logo.

● The first step is to select the object in front by clicking on it.

2 SENDING TO THE BACK

● Drop down the **Arrange** menu from the Menu bar.

● Click on **Send to Back**.

3 REORDERED LAYERS

● The name has been placed on the lower level of the two objects and now no longer obscures the logo.

PAPER SIZE

It is best to make sure you are working on the correct page size from the outset. The work you have already done may not fit if you have to reduce the paper size later. Also, you may have more space than you intended if you have to increase the size.

1 OPENING PRINT SETUP

● To change the paper size begin by clicking on **File** on the Menu bar and select **Print Setup**.

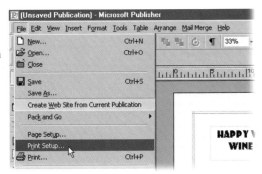

2 CHANGING THE PAPER SIZE

● The **Print Setup** dialog box opens.
● Click on the arrow to the right of the **Paper Size:** panel to drop down the paper size menu.
● Select the correct paper size and click on **OK**.

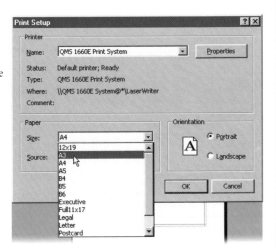

● Your paper size has been changed.
● This may affect your work: you may have to redesign your page, add more pages, or shift material onto other pages.

INSERTING NEW PAGES

Unless your publication is a single-sided, single-page document, you will need to add a new page at some point. You may be familiar with Word automatically adding a new page when necessary, but Publisher needs to be told when to add a page.

1 INSERTING A PAGE
● Click on **Insert** on the Menu bar, then **Page** to open the **Insert Page** dialog box.

● The choices to make include the number of new pages, where the new page(s) is to be placed, and whether you want the new page(s) to be blank, contain one text frame, or duplicate all the contents of the current page.
● Click on **OK** when done.

2 REMOVING PAGES

● If you want to remove a page, display it, and drop down the **Edit** menu.
● Click on **Delete Page**.
● The page is now deleted from your publication.

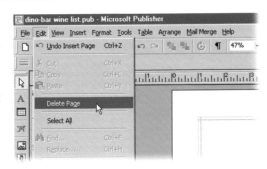

PAGE NUMBERS

Remember to leave some space in a corner or at an edge of your page, for page numbers. Page numbers are placed on the *background* part of your document (see box below), where any entry is repeated on every page of your publication.

1 GO TO THE BACKGROUND

● First, drop down the **View** menu.
● Click on **Go to Background**.
● You are now viewing the background of your page.

FOREGROUND AND BACKGROUND

For the majority of the time when you are using Publisher, you are looking at the *foreground* view of your publication. There is also another view of each page, called the *background*. The background is always the same for each page, and contains any text or graphics that are to appear on every page (or on every odd or even page) of your publication, for example, the page numbers. You can navigate between background view and foreground view by using the **View** menu (see Step 1 above).

2 INSERTING PAGE NUMBERS

● Create a text frame with the text frame tool.

● Select the frame and add any accompanying text.

● Drop down the **Insert** menu and click on **Page Numbers** to insert them.

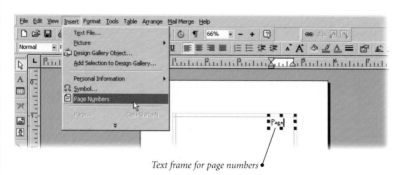

Text frame for page numbers ●

TEXT FRAME MARGINS AND COLUMNS

An important part of laying out your pages is to make sure that your text is clearly visible and properly laid out within the text frames. You can use columns and margins to control the layout of the text frames on your page.

1 ADJUSTING THE MARGINS

● Select the text frame and click **Text Frame Properties** in the **Format** menu. The **Text Frame Properties** dialog box opens.

● Adjust each of the frame's margins by using the spin buttons.

● When you have finished, click on **OK**.

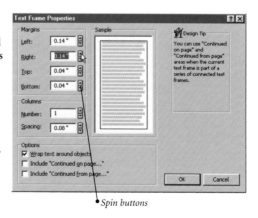

● *Spin buttons*

2 ADDING COLUMNS

● To add columns, select the text frame, and display the **Text Frame Properties** dialog box as in Step 1.

● Adjust the number of columns by using the spin buttons next to **Number:**.

● You can see a preview in the **Sample** box.

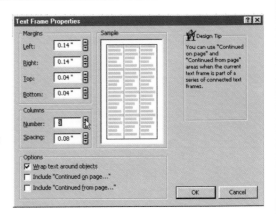

3 ADJUST COLUMN SPACING

● Increase or decrease the spacing between the columns by using the spin buttons next to **Spacing:**.

● When you have finished, click on **OK** and your columns have been created.

● If you are not happy with the readability of your text after you have created columns, return to the **Text Frame Properties** dialog box and increase the spacing between the columns.

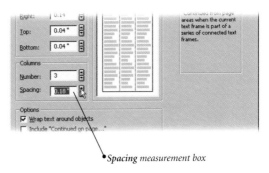

Spacing measurement box

LITERATURE

'Nature' at the fin-de-siècle — an uneasy orde

The concept of Nature, a culturally recognised and shared order with claim to universal as well as social scope, is a contentious one charged with political, social, scientific, aesthetic and philosophical implications. A striking characteristic of the fin de siècle is its breaking away from Victorian values and rejec-

uneasily into the late Almighty's shoes. A materialist vision of the universe became the conventional view:

John is practical in the extreme. He has no patience with faith, an intense horror of superstition, and he scoffs openly at any talk of

response to this need mysticism, the occult metaphysics, as well influence of philosopl from other cultures, emerged from or were sucked into the spiritu vacuum in the post-Darwinian Western w Significantly, in a liter context, aesthetics its became (for certain a

WORKING WITH TEXT

Sharpening your techniques by changing fonts, aligning text, and using font effects, will give your whole publication a crisper, more creative, professional-looking edge.

ALTERING FONT AND SIZE

The choice of fonts is possibly the most essential element affecting the design and feel of your publication. The golden rule is to keep fonts simple – too much variety in the styles and sizes can make your design appear frivolous and even unreadable.

1 SELECTING THE TEXT

● Using the mouse, highlight the text that you want to format.
● If you want to highlight all the text in a text frame (and all text frames connected to it 🖰), hold down the Ctrl key on your keyboard and press **A**.

Highlighted text ●

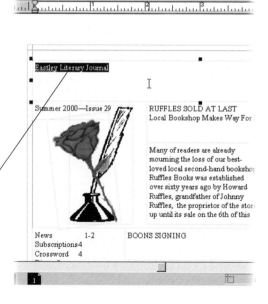

2 CHOOSING A FONT

● Click on the arrow to the right of the **Font** box on the toolbar.

● Scroll through the drop-down menu until you find the font you want.

● Click once on your chosen font.

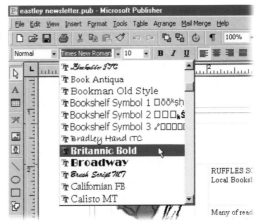

3 FONT SIZE

● To change the font size of your selected text, click on the arrow to the right of the **Font Size** box.

● Click on the point size you require in the drop-down menu.

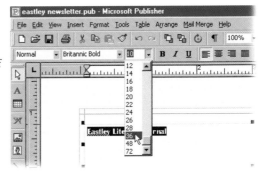

4 THE FONT DIALOG BOX

● You can change all the attributes of your current font by using the **Font** dialog box.

● Drop down the **Format** menu and click on **Font**.

● The **Font** dialog box appears. You can adjust the font, the font size, and font style in this dialog box.
● You can also change styles that include, for example, small capitals, underlines, and shadows.

ALIGNMENT AND TABS

We have already dealt with aligning objects on your page ⌐. Now, let's look at aligning the text within your text frames. You can align your text to the left or the right side of the frame, center it, or justify it so that the left and right ends of the lines are even instead of being ragged down one side. You can also set tabs so that the first word of each item in a list is placed precisely below the one above.

1 CENTERING TEXT

● Using the mouse, select the line or lines of text that you want to center.
● Click on the **Center** button on the toolbar.

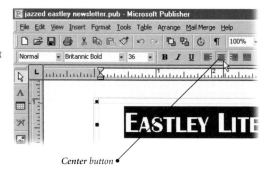

Center button ●

2 JUSTIFYING TEXT

● Select the text you want to justify.

● If you want to highlight all the text in a text frame (and all text frames connected to it), click on the frame, hold the [Ctrl] key and press A.

● Click on the **Justify** button on the toolbar.

Justify button

3 USING TABS TO MAKE COLUMNS

● First, select the text (typically a tabbed list) for which you need to set tabs.

● Click on the part of the ruler where you want your tab positioned. You can drag tabs with the mouse to reposition them.

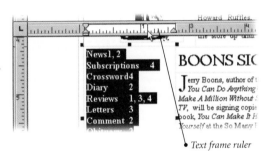

● *Text frame ruler*

4 CREATING CUSTOM TABS

● You can change the settings of your tabs, for example, to place a row of dots, or a *tab leader*, between the two columns.

● Click on **Format** on the Menu bar and select **Tabs** to open the **Tabs** dialog box on screen.

5 SELECTING THE TYPE OF TAB

● The tabs you have set are listed in the **Tab stop position:** box. Select the tab you want to work on by clicking on it in the box.

● In the **Alignment** section, select the text alignment that you want the tabbed list to adopt – left, centered, right, or decimal.

● Select the leader – the dots, dashes, lines, or bullets that will lead from one column to the next.

● Click on **OK**.

● Your tabs now have the alignment and leader that have been set.

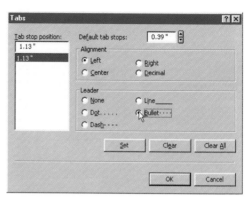

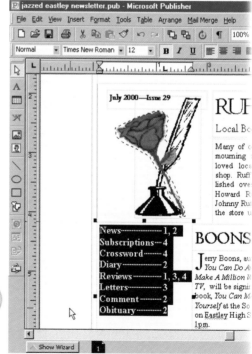

DROP CAPS

You can open the first paragraph of a story in your publication by using a dropped capital letter, known as a *drop*

cap, which is a single character – much larger than the rest – that starts a paragraph, and adds style to your text.

1 ADDING A DROP CAP

● Place the insertion point in the first paragraph.
● Click on **Format** on the Menu bar and select **Drop Cap** to open the **Drop Cap** dialog box.

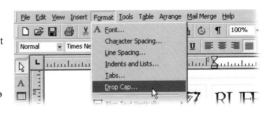

2 CHOOSING A DROP CAP

● The first tab of the **Drop Cap** dialog box offers you various preset drop caps.
● Either choose one or click the **Custom Drop Cap** tab to make your own.
● Adjust the settings, such as, which font to use for the drop cap, how many letters high it should be, and its position in relation to the rest of the text.
● Click on **OK**.
● Your chosen drop cap is now included in your text.

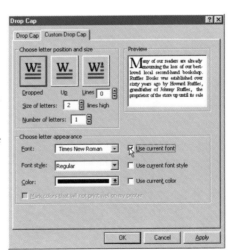

Drop cap •

Many of our readers are already mourning the loss of our best-loved local second-hand

6th of this month.
Mr Ruffles is said to have been forced to close the business due to

USING WORDART

Although, as we have seen, there are many ways in which regular text can be manipulated in Publisher, sometimes you may need special effects to make a particular heading really stand out.

Publisher includes a feature called WordArt, which allows you to be highly creative with your text. Once again, simplicity is vital to good design – it's always best not to overdo the frills.

1 REPLACING THE TEXT FRAME

● If you have already typed the text in a text frame that you want to add special effects to, you will have to remove it. WordArt is treated differently and separately from regular text.

● Select the old text frame, and right-click on it.

● A menu pops up in which you can click on **Delete Object**.

2 ADDING A WORDART FRAME

● Click on the **WordArt** button near the top of the **Objects** toolbar.

● Draw your WordArt frame onto the page so that it has the size and shape that you want.

●*WordArt button*

3 ENTERING YOUR TEXT

● The WordArt frame appears together with the **Enter Your Text Here** dialog box in which you can enter your text.

● Click on **Update Display** to insert your text in the WordArt frame.

● The WordArt toolbar replaces the Publisher toolbars when working with WordArt.

4 STRETCHING YOUR TEXT

● The **Stretch** button can change the shape of your text to fit the frame.

● Click on it once to turn the stretch feature on.

● Click on it again to turn the feature off.

Stretch button ●

5 CHANGING THE WORDART SHAPE

● Click on the arrow to the right of the **Shape** box to view the Shape palette.

● Click on a shape to choose the shape of your WordArt text.

● To return your text to normal, click on the top left box in the palette.

● Your WordArt shape is now changed.

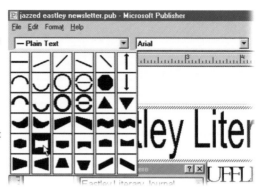

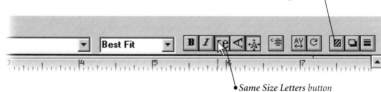

6 SAME SIZE LETTERS

● This feature equalizes the size of all letters, both upper and lower case.

● To make use of this effect, click on the **Same Size Letters** button.

● To turn it off, click on the button again.

Shading button ●

●*Same Size Letters button*

7 ROTATING YOUR TEXT

● We dealt with rotating objects earlier ◻. This feature rotates the text within the WordArt frame.

● Click on the **Rotate** button to open the **Special Effects** dialog box.

● You can use the **Rotation** box to rotate the text, and the **Slider** box to change the slant of the characters.

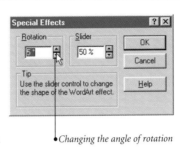

Changing the angle of rotation

8 SHADING YOUR TEXT

● You can change both the color and pattern of your text using the **Shading** dialog box.

● Click on the **Shading** button to bring it up.

● Choose on a pattern under **Style**, and drop down the **Color** menu to choose a color.

● Click on **Apply** and then on **OK** to quit editing your WordArt.

● Click anywhere on the page outside the WordArt frame to see the effect.

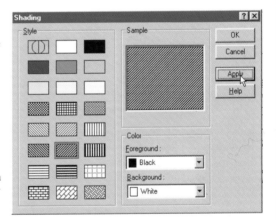

◻ **27** **Rotating an Image**

FINAL TOUCHES

Prior to printing, there are a number of ways in which you can enhance the appearance of your publication. In this section we add some finishing touches to a publication.

BORDERS AND SHADOWS

To emphasize an object, such as a picture or a text frame, we can add a border around the edges to make it stand out. You can use a border that has a single line, or use Publisher's BorderArt for more elaborate borders. If you give the frame a shadow as well, it will make the frame far more prominent on the page.

1 ADDING A BORDER

● With the cursor in a text frame, click on **Line/Border Style** on the toolbar to drop down the menu.

● Choose one of the borders on the menu, or click on **More Styles**.

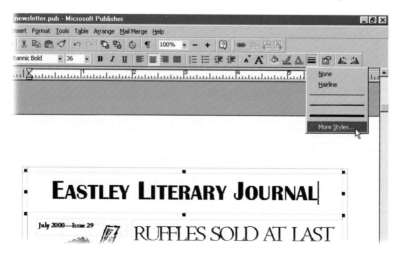

2 LINE BORDERS

● The **Border Style** dialog box opens. The **Line Border** tab contains the most commonly used line-based borders.
● Click on one of the boxes under **Choose a thickness** to select a line to use.
● To limit your border, click on a side that is not to have a border in the **Select a side** preview box, and then click on **None**.

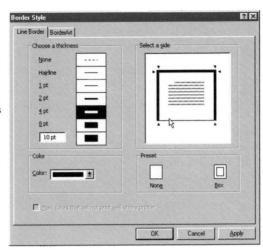

3 PUBLISHER'S BORDERART

● Click on the second tab to view the options available under **BorderArt**.
● Choose a border design from those in the **Available Borders** menu.
● Select the size in the **Border size:** box.
● When you have finished, click on **OK**.

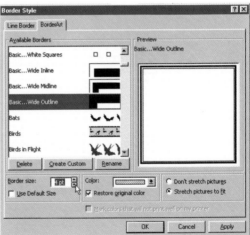

4 ADDING A SHADOW

● To add a shadow to your object, click on **Format** in the Menu bar and click on **Shadow** in the menu.

● Your object now has a border and a shadow.

● To remove the shadow, choose **Shadow** from the **Format** menu again. This turns the shadow off.

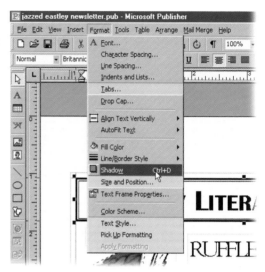

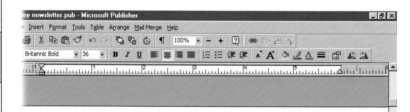

Colors

Color can be applied to various parts of your publication. Text frames and WordArt frames can be filled with a background color, borders and shadows surrounding them can be colored, and the text in frames can also be in color.

1 ADDING A BACK-GROUND COLOR

● Select the text frame that you want to fill with a background color.
● Click on the **Fill Color** button on the toolbar to drop down the **Fill Color** menu of options.
● Click on **More Colors** to open the **Colors** dialog box.

2 SELECTING ALL COLORS

The **Colors** dialog box opens. Click on the **All colors** radio button to see the full range of available colors.

3 CHOOSING A COLOR

● Click on the area of the color map that most closely matches the required color.
● Move the shade slider to lighten or darken the selected color.
● Click on **OK** when you have arrived at the correct color setting.

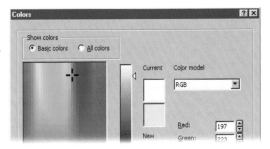

4 THE COMPLETED BACKGROUND

● The **Colors** dialog box closes and the selected color is now the background of the text box.

5 ADDING A FILL EFFECT

● If you want a more sophisticated color wash behind your text, you can use a **Fill Effect**.

● Click on the **Fill Color** button on the toolbar to drop down the **Fill Color** menu.

● Click on **Fill Effects** to open the **Fill Effects** dialog box on screen.

6 SELECTING A GRADIENTS FILL

● In the **Fill Effects** dialog box, click on the **Gradients** radio button.

● The previously chosen background color is shown in the two color boxes in the **Color** section. Click on the arrow to the right of the **Color 2:** box and select a related color to provide the gradient for the background.

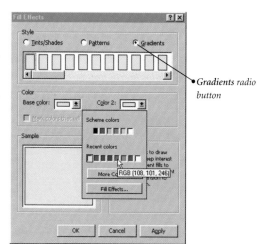

●*Gradients radio button*

7 SELECTING A GRADIENT STYLE

● Select a particular gradient from the gallery in the Style section. The effect is shown in the Sample pane.

● Click on **OK** when you have finished.

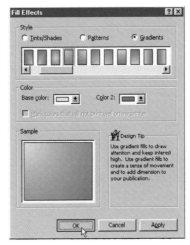

8 CHANGING THE FONT COLOR

● You may want to give your text a specific color too. Begin by selecting the text to be changed.

● Click on the **Font Color** button to display the **Font Color** menu.

● Select a color by clicking on it. Click on **OK** to complete your color changes.

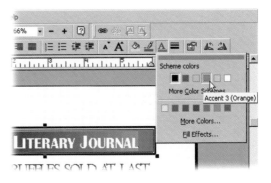

9 THE FINAL EFFECT

● Finally, click off the text box to see the final effect of the gradient and the chosen text color.

PRINTING

Because Publisher is designed to develop material for publishing, the time will come when you need to print on your own printer or through a commercial printing service.

PRINTING ON A DESKTOP PRINTER

Printing on your own printer is convenient, flexible and, for low-volume print runs, is very cost-effective. For higher volumes, and if the output quality of your printer is sufficient, you can print masters that can be used by a copy shop.

1 PRINTING YOUR PUBLICATION

● Make sure your printer is switched on and connected.
● Click on **File** in the Menu bar. Select **Print** to open the **Print** dialog box.

INKJET QUALITY

To achieve the highest quality printing from your inkjet printer, select **Options** from the **Tools** menu, click on the **Print** tab, and click in the **Print line-by-line** check box. This setting will improve printing, but may slow down your printer.

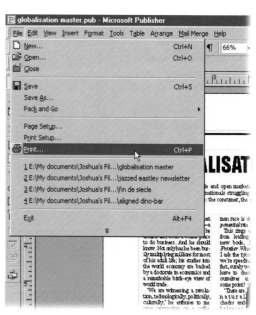

2 THE PRINT DIALOG BOX

● Here you can adjust how many copies of the publication to print and, if necessary, which pages.

● To print one high quality copy, simply click **OK**, but before doing that you may wish to alter other options. Many are available through the printer properties dialog box, which is opened by clicking on **Properties**.

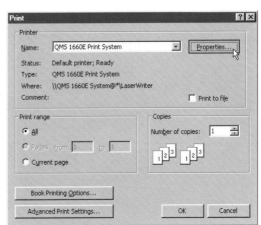

3 THE PRINTER PROPERTIES BOX

● One of the important options available in the printer properties dialog box is how many pages of your publication are to be printed on one page. This is especially useful if you have used a template for folded publications.

● In the **Layout** section you can select how your publication appears on the printed page.

● Click on **OK** when the layout is correct to return to the **Print** dialog box.

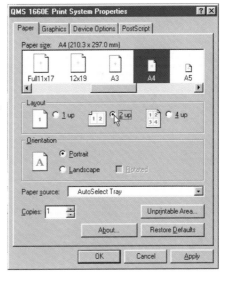

● To alter the print quality settings, click on **Advanced Print Settings**.

4 PRINTING WITH- OUT GRAPHICS

● The **Print Settings** dialog box opens. If you want to run off a quick draft, without printing the image files in your publication, click on **Do not print any graphics**.

● Click on the **Device Options** tab for a further range of print settings.

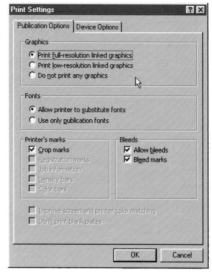

5 CHANGING THE RESOLUTION

● In the **Device Options** tab, drop down the **Resolution** menu.

● You can select a print resolution (how many dots per inch) from the menu.

● When you have finished, click on **OK**.

● In the **Print** dialog box, click on **OK**.

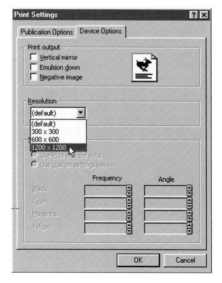

● The **Printing** progress panel opens where the progress of the print job is monitored by a progress bar. Your publication will soon be printed out.

PACKING FILES FOR A PRINT SERVICE

For the highest resolution printing, a large number of copies, or for good quality color, you may decide that your desktop printing facilities are not good enough and that you need to use a commercial printing service. If you do, Publisher can pack your publication onto a floppy disk so it is ready to use by a printing service.

1 USING PACK AND GO
● Click on **File** on the Menu bar.

● In the drop-down **File** menu, select **Pack and Go** by clicking on it.
● In the submenu that opens to the side of the main menu, click on the **Take to a Commercial Printing Service** option.

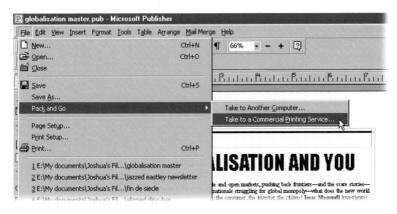

2 THE PACK AND GO WIZARD

● The **Pack and Go Wizard** dialog box opens listing the operations that can be carried out.

● Click on the **Next** button.

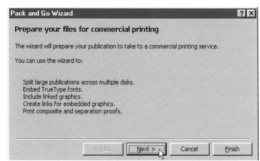

3 CHOOSING A FILE LOCATION

● The wizard prompts you to choose a location for your packed files.

● Choose **A:** to put the files on a floppy disk (make sure there is one present in the drive).

● Click on the **Next** button in the dialog box.

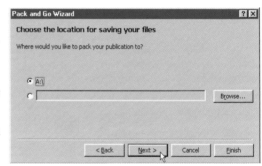

4 INCLUDE FONTS AND GRAPHICS

● So that the printing service can make use of the fonts and images you have used in your publication, the wizard can include them on your disk.

● Make sure all the boxes are checked.

● Click on the **Next** button.

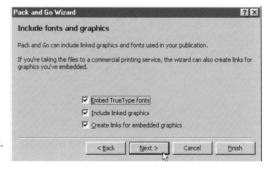

5 PACKING YOUR PUBLICATION

● The wizard's steps are now completed.

● Click on the **Finish** button to pack your publication for printing.

● A progress panel is provided for you to monitor the packing process. This is not particularly important for small publications, but can be essential to monitor the packing of a very large publication.

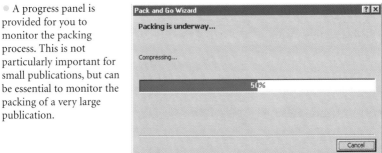

● Your publication has been packed.

● Read the dialog box for instructions on how to use your packed files.

● Click on **OK**.

QUICK PUBLICATIONS

Although Publisher has the flexibility to let you create your own completely original publications, sometimes it's quicker to use an off-the-shelf design and tailor it to suit your needs.

USING WIZARDS

Wizards are a quick, easy way to make a variety of good-looking publications. Here, we work through a typical wizard.

Remember, each wizard is slightly different, as each one is designed to help you with a different type of publication.

1 SETTING UP WIZARDS

● Before you start to use Publisher's wizards, make sure that the options are set up to let you use them.
● Click on **Tools** in the Menu bar and click on **Options**. The **Options** dialog box opens.

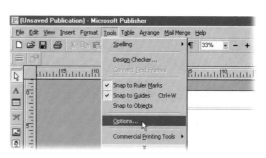

● Make sure there are checkmarks in the **Use Quick Publication Wizard for blank publications** check box, and in the **Step through wizard questions** check box.

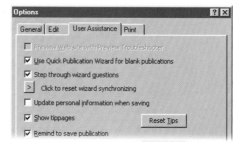

● Click on **OK** when you are happy with the settings.

2 OPENING A NEW FILE
● To begin, click on **File** on the Menu bar and then select **New** from the drop-down menu.

3 CHOOSING A WIZARD
● There are wizards for different publications.

Click on the type of wizard you need from the list of wizards on the left of the screen display.

● Choose a design that suits your needs from the larger display window.
● Click on **Start Wizard**.

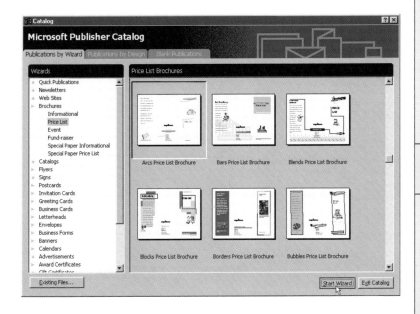

4 CHOOSING BY DESIGN

● Alternatively, you can choose your wizard by design – click the **Publications by Design** tab.

● Select your preferred design from the **Design Sets** list at left of the screen.

● Choose a design from the larger display window.

● Click on **Start Wizard**.

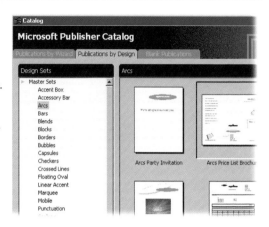

5 THE WIZARD'S STEP OPTIONS

● Your design will appear on the screen and the wizard's dialog box is at left of the screen.

● Click **Next** to move to the start of the options.

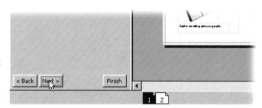

6 CHOOSING A COLOR SCHEME

● The wizard prompts you to choose a color scheme.

● Select the one you think is the most appropriate.

● Click on **Next**.

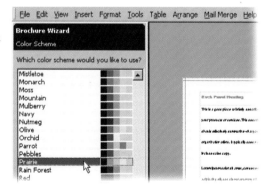

7 ADDRESS PLACEHOLDER

● The wizard asks you if you want to include a placeholder for you customers' addresses.
● Choose **Yes** or **No**.
● Click on **Next**.

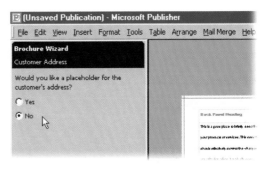

8 ADDING AN ORDER FORM

● The wizard asks if you want an order form in your publication and, if so, which type.
● Select an **Order Form**, or **None**.
● Click on **Next**.

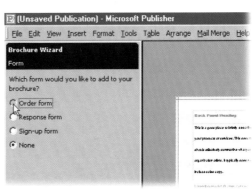

9 PERSONAL INFORMATION

● The wizard asks which set of personal information you would like to be included. Select a set and click on **Update**.

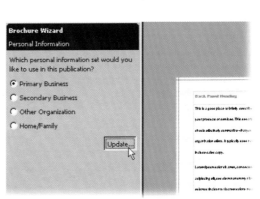

● A **Personal Information** dialog box opens for you to complete. Enter the details and click on **Update**.

● That is the last of the wizard's questions, so click on **Finish** when you are returned to the wizard.

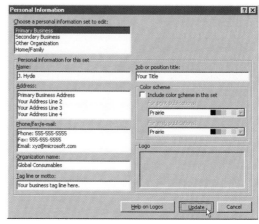

● If you create a feature on your publication, Publisher will prompt you to check the wizard's work.

● If you wish, turn to the page using the page icons and have a look.

10 HIDING THE WIZARD

● When the wizard has finished, it stays open so that you can change any of the settings – you can even change the design.

● When you want to start work, click on **Hide Wizard** to create more workspace.

● When the wizard is hidden, you can bring it back by clicking on the **Show Wizard** button.

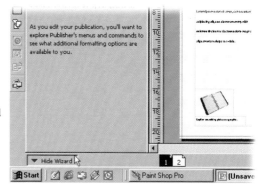

11 ADDING YOUR OWN WORK

● Replace the text in the publication with your own to make the publication specific to your needs.

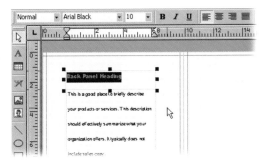

● Change the images as required. You can do this by using **Picture** from the **Format** menu.
● You can also format your text and objects. Every element in the publication can be changed.

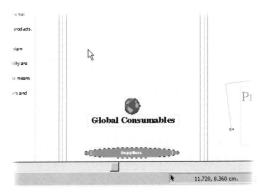

12 SAVE YOUR PUBLICATION

● When you have reworked the publication, save it 📄.
● In the **Save As** dialog box, choose a file name for your publication and click on the **Save** button.

📄 **Saving Your**
15 **Publication**

USING TEMPLATES

You can make your own ready-made solutions, too. If you edit a regular publication, such as a newsletter, you will need to design and store a basic prototype model for all issues. This prototype will contain only the frames and objects that are to appear in each issue. This prototype is known as a template.

1 SETTING UP A TEMPLATE

● You can create a template from a publication that contains elements and layouts to be reused.

● First, remove the text and objects that will change from one issue to the next. Leave the regular features.

● When you have finished, your publication is an outline structure, which is ready to be filled with the content of the next issue.

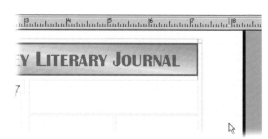

2 SAVING YOUR TEMPLATE

● Click on **File** in the Menu bar and click on **Save As**. Avoid clicking on **Save** as this will overwrite the old publication.

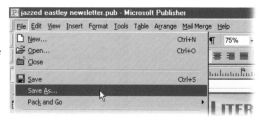

● In the **Save As** dialog box, type a file name for your template.

● Click on the arrow at right of the **Save as type** box to drop down the list of options and choose **Publisher Template**.

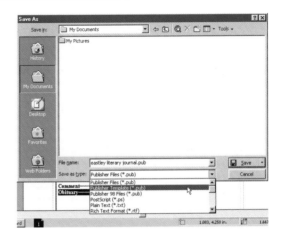

3 USING YOUR TEMPLATE

● When you need to use your template, you can open it from the **Catalog** dialog box.

● Click on **File** on the Menu bar, and click on **New** to open the **Catalog** dialog box.

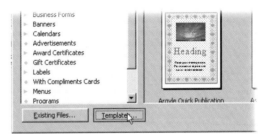

● Click on the **Templates** button and the **Open Template** dialog box opens.

● Select your template from the list.

● Click on the **Open** button and you can create a new issue, which must be saved using the **Save As** option in the **File** menu.

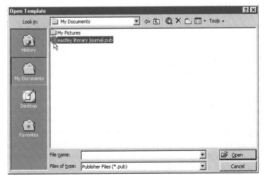

GLOSSARY

ALIGNMENT
Objects can be lined up with each other on the page or with the margins. This is called alignment. Text frames can also be aligned horizontally or vertically on the page.

BACKGROUND AND FOREGROUND
Most of what you place in your publication is on the foreground of the page. There is also a background, which is identical for each page (or pair of facing pages), in which you can insert page numbers and other elements that you wish to be repeated.

BORDER
A line or pattern around a frame. You can choose from a wide range of patterned borders, which are available by using BorderArt.

BULLETS
Black, filled-in circles that signify points in a list, or which can be used as tab leaders.

CROPPING
If you trim your images – or even show only a small detail of the original – this is known as cropping the image.

DROP CAP
A dropped capital letter is where the first letter in a paragraph is larger than the following text to mark the beginning of a new story.

FONT
A typeface in which your text is shown on the page.

GRADIENT FILL
A wash of color that fills an object, in which the color fades from lighter to darker.

GROUP (OF OBJECTS)
You can join several objects together to form one group. The group can then be moved and formatted as a single object.

KERNING
Adjusting the space between two individual characters.

LANDSCAPE
Horizontal page orientation: the page is broader than it is tall.

LAYERING
The system by which Publisher decides which object goes in front of any other object with which it shares space on the page.

NUMBERING
You can add automated numbers to each item in a list: this is called numbering.

PICTURE FRAME
An object on the Publisher page that can contain graphics.

PORTRAIT
Upright page orientation: the page is taller than it is wide.

SHADOW
A darker strip on the page, beneath an object.

STORY
An entire passage of text. The passage does not have to be continuous because two text frames can be connected so that the text of the story flows from one to the other.

TAB LEADER
A row of dots, dashes, or bullets between, for example, chapter titles aligned down the left-hand side of a table of contents to the corresponding page numbers aligned down the right.

TEMPLATE
A ready-made design containing basic elements of, for example, text, objects, and formatting that you can add to and amend to create a publication. You can create your own templates and save them.

TEXT FRAME
An object on the Publisher page designed to contain text. Like all frames it does not print out; it acts as a guide for the placing of text on your screen.

TRACKING
Adjusting the spaces between all the characters in a selected block of text.

WIZARD
A mini-program that is part of Publisher that guides you through a process, such as the creation of a specific type of new publication.

WORDART
A tool for creating colorful, lively and distinctive headings or logos.

WRAPPING
If you wrap your text around an image, the text flows into the space around the image and follows its shape closely.

INDEX

ACKNOWLEDGMENTS

PUBLISHER'S ACKNOWLEDGMENTS
Dorling Kindersley would like to thank the following:
Paul Mattock of APM, Brighton, for commissioned photography.
Microsoft Corporation for permission to reproduce screens
from within Microsoft® Publisher 2000.

Every effort has been made to trace the copyright holders.
The publisher apologizes for any unintentional omissions and would be pleased,
in such cases, to place an acknowledgment in future editions of this book.

Microsoft is a registered trademark of Microsoft Corporation
in the United States and/or other countries.